Anjum Altaf is Ambreen's brother, whom I know slightly

Transgressions

Poems Inspired by Faiz Ahmed Faiz

Anjum Altaf

Published by
LG PUBLISHERS DISTRIBUTORS
49, Lane No. 14, Pratap Nagar
Mayur Vihar Phase I, Delhi 110 091
Tel : 011 2279 5641 email: lgpdist@gmail.com

Typeset at
Arpit Printographers, Delhi

Printed at
D.K. Fine Art Press, Delhi 110 052

*for my parents
from whom I inherited
the love of poetry*

Contents

By Way of Explanation

On November 13, 2015, after the Stade de France bombings in Paris, Brussels went into a three-day lockdown. The incongruity of the news made me think of an Urdu poem, a verse from *Observe the City from Here* by Faiz Ahmed Faiz: "The city walls stretch/Like a prison in all directions."[1] It was a poem from many decades ago, far from Europe and its discontents, far from terrorism and its retributions, yet speaking to the present. The lines kept resonating in my mind, and I jotted a sort of update to them in English.

Three months later, there was news from closer to home, less gruesome but still significant: intolerant mobs had assaulted students at Jawaharlal Nehru University in Delhi. Thinking about them called up some lines from Faiz again: "My body is in tatters/Pieces of it flutter in the wind like pennants."[2] Once more, I found myself making notes in the margins. I realized then that something more was going on than just a recall of memory.

It is a typical reaction in our part of the world, still steeped in a culture of orality, to recall poetry that speaks to any given situation. For wisdom and wit we turn to Ghalib, for love to Mir, for faith to Iqbal, for lamentation to Sauda, for the rejection of hypocrisy to Bulleh Shah, Nanak and Kabir. For resistance and hope, we turn to Faiz. This

---

1. Translated by Baran Farooqi, 2017.
2. Translated by Khalid Hasan, 2006.

is, however, a more contextual subject matter: history repeats itself, but not very neatly, and hopes rarely play out as desired. The poetry of resistance needs to be constantly refreshed to make it speak to our times. That, perhaps, was what I was doing unconsciously while scribbling in the margins of Faiz—not just recalling lines or translating them but engaging with them to make them congruent with the present.

Consider the last lines of Faiz's reflection, *Dawn of Freedom,* on the creation of Pakistan in 1947—'Let us go on, our goal is not reached yet.'[3] Or the stirring response—'We shall overcome'—to the dictatorship of Zia ul Haq in 1979. What solace would Faiz offer for the dashed hopes and where would he direct us now?

The absence of equally powerful poetry after Faiz underscores a problem peculiar to Urdu—that it is past its peak as a medium for the expression of lasting literary feelings. For a brief interlude in the mid-nineteenth century the language of the North Indian aristocracy shifted from Persian to a vernacular of which Urdu was a composite part. That was the golden age of Urdu poetry. But unlike, say, the Russian aristocracy that switched from French to the language of the people for good, the North Indian aristocracy abandoned the native language for English within a few generations.

It is impossible to conceive that Urdu will see the likes of Ghalib, Mir or Sauda again and it is only its twilight that has given us Iqbal and Faiz. This explains the fact that more than thirty years after his death Faiz remains for us the touchstone of the poetry of sustenance in Urdu with no

---

3. Translated by Khalid Hasan, 2006.

replacement in sight. Indeed, it appears very unlikely that we will see the same quality of poetry in Urdu during our lives.

This would not have been a complete loss if a new generation of poets had filled the gap by writing in English but that is nowhere the case. Nor is it realistic to expect a flowering from planting a foreign seed in alien soil and so grossly neglecting its nurture. As a result, we are bereft and stranded in a desolate emotional terrain where many of us can neither adequately comprehend in Urdu nor quite express ourselves sufficiently in English.

What then is to be done? Frankly, I have no answer to this crippling state nor did I comprehend it fully when I leant on Faiz to scribble some lines in English. All I can do is offer what I have borrowed and reworked as a tribute to a major poet of our times.

Lahore
January 2018

Anjum Altaf

Acknowledgements

My deepest debt is to my parents to whom I have dedicated this volume. My love of Urdu poetry is due to my mother and my introduction to English literature owes much to my father.

The engagement with Faiz was nurtured in almost daily conversations with my wife and sons over decades. Samia knows a lot of Faiz by heart, Kabir has sung Faiz in public numerous times, and I am pleased to include in this volume Hasan's personal tribute to Faiz which describes the nature of that engagement and its relevance to our lives.

These poems were not intended for publication and the credit or the blame for doing so is due to Professor Harbans Mukhia. He was among the very few with whom I shared some of the early efforts (because of his association with Jawaharlal Nehru University) and was pleasantly surprised by his insistence that I had something worthwhile to offer to a wider audience.

Syed Abbas Raza and Jim Culleny provided additional encouragement by accepting with enthusiasm a few of the early poems for publication on their wonderful website - *3 Quarks Daily*.

Articles by Tim Parks in *The New York Review of Books* motivated two of the poems. I am grateful to him for his generous acknowledgements.

Of course, the ultimate debt is to Faiz himself. In every life there are a few individuals who, at various junctures, change the trajectory of one's thinking. Faiz was such a person who entered my life somewhere in the first years of college amidst the intellectual turmoil of the Vietnam War. I still draw on him after all these years even as I engage with the poetry much more critically than I did as a student mesmerized by the vision of a better world.

Notes on Poems

Faiz Ahmed Faiz is considered among the most popular modern poets of Urdu. The poems in this collection are inspired by his poetry. Each poem corresponds to one by Faiz but is not a translation of it. Rather, it reflects my thoughts on the theme of the poem whose recall was often triggered by a contemporary event. Some of the resulting poems are close to the original, others ask questions of the poet, and a few engage with the argument. The resulting poems could be better considered transgressions rather than translations.

This choice was motivated by a desire to converse with Faiz while leaning on him to address universal concerns but it is also an indirect acknowledgement of the challenge posed by translating poetry, something Faiz himself articulated clearly:

> Translating poetry, even when confined to a cognate language with some formal and idiomatic affinities with the original compositions, is an exacting task, but this task is obviously far more formidable when the languages involved are far removed from each other in cultural background, rhythmic and formal patterns, and the vocabulary of symbol and allusion as Urdu and English.[1]

---

1. In Khalid Hasan, ed., *O City of Lights: Faiz Ahmed Faiz - Selected Poetry and Biographical Notes*, Oxford University Press, 2006. The reader interesting in understanding the pitfalls in translating poetry from Urdu to English would benefit from reading 'On

Because the poems are not translations and the intended audience is one of readers unfamiliar with Urdu I have not included the Urdu text of Faiz's original poems. Urdu speakers don't need to read Faiz in English when they have access to the much richer originals.[2]

One feature of Urdu poetry I have retained is its minimal use of punctuation which reflects the fact that Urdu poetry is meant to be heard and not read. For readers it creates a multiplicity of meanings depending on how they engage with the text thereby making them active participants in the interaction. I have found this ambiguity a creative device for experimentation.

Each poem in this collection is followed by notes that include the following:

The name in Urdu of the original poem by Faiz.[3]

An indication if an English translation of the poem is included in any of the following volumes:

Poems by Faiz translated by Victor Kiernan, Vanguard Books, Lahore, Undated.

Faiz Ahmed Faiz: The Rebel's Silhouette translated from Urdu by Agha Shahid Ali, Oxford India Paperbacks, New Delhi, 1991.

O City of Lights: Faiz Ahmed Faiz—Selected Poetry and Biographical Notes selected and edited by Khalid Hasan with translations

---

Not Translating Hafez' by Dick Davis (accessible at http://cat.middlebury.edu/~nereview/25-1-2/Davis.html) which deals with Persian, a language with close affinity to Urdu.

2. For the determined reader, however, the originals of almost all the poems—in Urdu, Devanagari and Roman scripts—are conveniently available at the excellent website rekhta.org.

3. In transliterating the names of the poems into English I have followed the convention of capitalising the letters that truly change the pronunciation of the word. These include the three retroflexes (Te, Daal, and Re), the letter Ghain, and the nasalized N. All other letters are represented as lower-case.

by Daud Kamal and Khalid Hasan, Oxford University Press, Karachi, 2006.

The True Subject: Selected Poems of Faiz Ahmed Faiz translated by Naomi Lazard, Oxford Pakistan Paperbacks, 2012.

The Best of Faiz translated by Shiv K. Kumar, Vintage, India, 2013.

Faiz Ahmed Faiz: The Colours of My Heart translated by Baran Farooqi, Penguin Books, India, 2017.

An acknowledgement if my rendering included in this volume has been first published elsewhere.

An explanation if a particular event was instrumental in my recall of the original poem by Faiz.

HASAN ALTAF

فیض کے نام

[Poet's note: I realize that some readers may be confused by the appearance of Urdu words in an otherwise English-language poem. These words are part of the poem, and since the poem is dedicated to Faiz, they are mostly words drawn from his poetry–"*faryādī*," "*rōshniyōñ kē shehr*," "*dard kē kāsnī pāzēb*," and of course the long quote from his poem "Ham Jō Tārīk Rāhōñ Mēñ Mārē Ga'ē." While I could have translated these words into English, it was very important for me to keep them in Urdu.

This poem is not really about Faiz but about what he represents for me. Growing up in America, Faiz's poetry was one of the strongest links I had to Pakistan and to Urdu. If I had not read and listened to his poetry as a child, it would have been much harder for me to acclimatize to Pakistan when my family moved back there when I was fourteen, and I would not be as attached to Pakistan as I now am. My connection to what I think of as 'home' is built on Faiz—he was like a bridge from my suburban childhood to something that was both in my past and in my future.

The main feeling I always got from Faiz's poetry was hope and dreams, and a desire to change things. Seeing Pakistan now, unchanged in so many ways, I wonder what Faiz would have to say, and I wonder what we who read him can offer to him or say to him. So the words from his poetry have to be in Urdu—partly because that is how I always think of them, partly because it was in Urdu that they connected me to Pakistan, but mostly because I think of them as questions, questions that I think Faiz would ask of us. In that sense, the English of the poem is my attempt at some kind of answer. That's what I was thinking as I put them in, and that is what I wanted for the reader to get from the poem.]

I remember finding you, buried there
    in the shrouds of dust and spiderwebs,
    in the back, in the dark.
The way your face shone from there as we lifted
    you out, the brilliant white of your words,
    like the sound of someone
        clearing their throat to sing against the stillness
    like a hand turning off the lights
    in a bright room.

I don't think I'd known you till then,
    فریادی for so long
    I don't think I knew the voice I heard before I was
    born, words reaching me like rhythm in sleep.
I don't think I ever knew your face,
    now on my wall, white on black against blankness
    and blocked windows.
The curve of your words like sweat on skin,
    like the trails of streetlights on glittering city nights,
    a nimbus.
    A path.

قتل گاہوں سے چن کر ہمارے علم
اور نکلیں گے عشاق کے قافلے
جن کی راہِ طلب سے ہمارے قدم
مختصر کر چلے درد کے فاصلے

The steps are still waiting
    but I don't know how to walk them,
    my feet so new and unfamiliar and far away, the flag
still lies there on the killing fields
    but who can pick it up now?
Now

کون لوٹے گا؟

to start us again along the path?

There is nothing for me to give you.
Everything is gone now, I wonder
if your boy's spirit still chases butterflies
in the lanes of old Sialkot,
if your verses
still ring from prison cells
if your heart
is somewhere still beating
in some other's chest,
if even now there lingers
in the dark of some cell
away from the world, where some soul lies
languishing the perfume of a bouquet brought there
by a stranger.

The flag raised and lowered,
the battle not won, not lost,
forgotten and left behind like the closing of your
eyes, what else was there?
The armies you never wanted to
raise have slipped away, faded
to words in old voices tired over wine,
a brief shape in the blue of cigarette smoke
before impatient hands wave it away.

What paths can I walk for you?
So far away now. I don't even speak your language.
Your words are like music for me,
a lullaby that soothes with just its sound.
What can I give you?
I who look at the world, the new world

and see nothing
but this

روشنیوں کے شہر

still dark, waiting for your light?

In my dreams
    I bear you a bouquet
    of all the things I want to say to you and never will.
The perfume of
      my bones still strong enough to lift a flag,
      my voice still here to sing,
         my words which ache to speak
         and stay silent.
    The sound of chains on city streets
        the celebration in every چھنک

of these درد کے کاسنی پازیب

    that I keep hidden. What do I know of them?
The sky is never truly dark here, yet
      once midnight strikes I stand in the halo of the
      streetlights, a dark shape against the white,
waiting.

November 2005.
From Patti Smith, "Mummer Love"

Faiz ke Naam

First published in the *Annual of Urdu Studies*, Vol. 23, 2008.

Access at: http://www.urdustudies.com/pdf/23/13HasanAltaf.pdf

Hasan Altaf wrote this poem as a 17-year old freshman at New York University. He had taken the iconic Faiz poster with him that had been a part of his home all his life. Retrieving the poster from his bags on arrival at NYU provided the motivation for the poem.

Poems

Why

Not even dogs
Go as quietly as these men

Battered and bruised
Idle and begging
Homeless and hearthless
Stabbing each other for scraps
Starving in silence

Why

What myth is it
That keeps you
Divided
Amongst yourselves
That keeps you
Blind
To your strength

NOTES ON WHY

Title of original: *kuttey*

Translations available in: Khalid Hasan, Victor Kiernan, Shiv Kumar

This version first published: 3 Quarks Daily, February 12, 2016

Personal Note: Reading an article on human agency made me think of this poem. I felt the oppressed ought no longer to be dependent on outsiders for awareness of their condition. For an elaboration, see: https://thesouthasianidea.wordpress.com/2015/12/30/faiz-3-a-twist-in-the-tail/

Resist

Cursing, hurling vile abuse
They came to tarnish, ravish, debase
Parade the tatters of our soul
As emblems of their rule

Hordes swarm the streets
Goose-stepping, flaunting steel
Threatening, intimidating those
Who dare refuse to kneel

We collect the shreds they tore
Dyed red in our blood
Sew them back in a banner
Bigger, brighter than before

NOTES ON RESIST

Title of original: *dar-e umiid ke daryuuza-gar*

Translations available in: Khalid Hasan

This version first published: *The South Asian Idea*, March 5, 2016

Personal Note: This poem came to mind following the attacks on the students and faculty of Jawaharlal Nehru University in 2016 and was dedicated to them. It was read by Professor Harbans Mukhia at the *Pratirodh* event at the Constitution Club in Delhi on April 9, 2016.

Speak

Now is the time to speak
Lips not sealed
Body unbroken
Blood coursing still
Through your veins

Now is the time to speak
Look
The iron glows red
Like your blood
The chain lies open
Like your lips

Now is the time to speak

Speak
For the tide of life runs out

Speak
For truth and honor shall not wait

Speak
Say all that needs be said today

NOTES ON SPEAK

Title of original: *bol*

Translations available in: Khalid Hasan, Victor Kiernan, Shiv Kumar, Baran Farooqi

This version first published: *The South Asian Idea*, March 6, 2016

Personal Note: The 2016 protests at Jawaharlal Nehru University in Delhi brought this poem to mind. It was published with a dedication to Kanhaiya Kumar, a leader of the student movement against curbs on freedom of speech.

Go

Unwept tears, inner torments
Enough
Hidden desires, silent accusations
Enough

Go
Flaunt your fetters in the street
Arms aloft, enraptured, intoxicated
Disheveled, blood stained
Go
Lovers are yearning for your love
Go

Tyrant and crowd
Await
Slings and stones
Await
Sorrows and failures
Await

Who else is left to love
But you
Who else is left to fight
But you
Who else is left to die
But you

Arise and go
For love's honour
Go

NOTES ON GO

Title of original: *aaj bazaar meiN pa ba jaulaaN chalo*

Translation available in: http://razarumi.com/aaj-bazaar-main-pa-ba-jolan-chalo-translated-explained/

This version first published: 3 Quarks Daily, February 23, 2017

Personal Note: There was a suicide bombing in Sehwan at the shrine of the sufi saint Lal Shahbaz Qalandar in February 2017. Sheema Kirmani, a symbol of defiance in Pakistan, went to perform at the shrine in the aftermath. This poem by Faiz came to mind and the adaptation was dedicated to Sheema - because she went. For the news coverage, see: https://images.dawn.com/news/1177132

Killing Fields

We followed you
In the killing fields
Enraptured
By the illusion of a promise

Consumed by the desire
To find you
Or lose ourselves
We made our homes
In the killing fields

Sweet was the seduction
To live to die for a promise

Knowing

Memories and desires
Shall cast
Again and again
Legions of lovers
In the killing fields

NOTES ON KILLING FIELDS

Title of original: *ham jo tareek raahoN meiN maarey gaye*

Translations available in: Agha Shahid Ali, Khalid Hasan

This version first published: Unpublished

Personal Note: This poem came to mind with the rise of fundamentalism and the ironic thought that there are people available and ready to follow to death any kind of charismatic leader.

Bangladesh

So often
I have said it to myself
I wish to say it to you
It should not be difficult
But it is

Do you sense
What I am trying to say
And
Why I cannot say it

Feelings are feelings
Words, words
So much is lost on the way

What would it take
To trust again
To feel
Without the need
To say

NOTES ON BANGLADESH

Title of original: *Dhaka se waapsii par*

Translations available in: Agha Shahid Ali, Khalid Hasan, Baran Farooqi

This version first published: *Economic and Political Weekly*, December 19, 2015

Personal Note: This poem, the one best known of Faiz's poems on the breakup of Pakistan, comes to mind every year in December, the month Bangladesh was liberated in 1971. It has a personal resonance for me as I was born in Dhaka. For an elaboration, see: https://thesouthasianidea.wordpress.com/2015/12/19/faiz-2-bangladesh-an-apriplum/

Beauty

Art, poetry
Strive for beauty

To bring alive
The henna on a hand
The anklet on a foot
To make immortal
A beloved's look
A lover's torment

This is my canvas
What I do best
With color and line
With rhythm and rhyme

Wait, you say
There are worlds
Beyond henna and anklet
Beyond lovers and beloveds
Pestilence, war, death, deprivation
Inequality, injustice, oppression, starvation
Will you not speak
Of such worlds

I hesitate
Afraid
With color and line
With rhythm and rhyme
To render them so beautiful
That looking over your shoulder
You might say
Guernica
Ah, what a lovely painting
And leaving
Pass me an Iliad
To enjoy on the way

NOTES ON BEAUTY

Title of original: *mauzu-e sukhan*

Translations available in: Victor Kiernan, Shiv Kumar

This version first published: Unpublished

Personal Note: This poem came to mind on reading an article titled 'Pretty Violence' by Tim Parks in which he asks whether there is any way to be free of the "aestheticizing process" involved in rendering ugly things in a beautiful manner. "I'm not sure there is," he answers. "*Guernica* is a beautiful painting. It has its wild glamour. But the painting is now more famous than the bombing it depicts and deplores, perhaps because it allows us to feel that being sophisticated and pacifist is one and the same. Which is gratifying. But there is no evidence it stopped any bombs."

http://www.nybooks.com/daily/2015/12/21/pretty-violence-david-shields-war-is-beautiful/

The adaptation of Faiz's poem was shared with Tim Parks in order to obtain his permission for publication.

The Cemetery in Leningrad

So many
Buried
In so few graves
The stones
Blank
Without names
No way to tell
Who lies where
Except
The flowers
Each intertwining
A loved one gone
With one
Unable to forget
And Mother Russia
Granite clad
Rosary in hand
Watching over all
With gratitude
And pride

NOTES ON THE CEMETERY IN LENINGRAD

Title of original: *Leningrad ka goristaan*

Translations available in: Naomi Lazard, Khalid Hasan

This version first published: Unpublished

Personal Note: This poem came to mind following the ceremonies for soldiers dying in the multiple wars in the Middle East and West Asia.

A Refugee in Paris

What do I know of this city
A migrant, a refugee
Carrying a storehouse of fears

Its splendor faded
In the failing light
Its steps sprouting
Tense, sinister shadows
Shrouded in suspicions

What do I know of this city
A stranger skirting light and shadows
Seeking a place to bury
Restless thoughts

NOTES ON A REFUGEE IN PARIS

Title of original: *Paris*

Translations available in: Naomi Lazard, Khalid Hasan, Shiv Kumar

This version first published: Unpublished

Personal Note: This poem came to mind on account of the growing refugee crisis in Europe and the events in Paris, in particular.

The City

Look
My city bedecks itself in fetters

The carefree walk
The careless talk

No more

The head held high
The feet unbound

No more

No more
I trust

Light from dark
Wine from blood
Joy from mourning

Flowers in my city
Wilt into the dust

NOTES ON THE CITY

Title of original: *yahaaN se sheher ko dekho*

Translations available in: Agha Shahid Ali, Naomi Lazard, Shiv Kumar, Baran Farooqi

This version first published: 3 Quarks Daily, November 30, 2015

Personal Note: I recalled this poem by Faiz when Brussels was locked down for three days following a terrorist attack in Paris. For an elaboration, see: https://thesouthasianidea.wordpress.com/2015/11/30/faiz-1-the-city/

Land of Unfulfilled Desires

When I encounter
The land of unfulfilled desires and hopeless expectations
I cannot bear to look that way
I tell myself I must flee
Escape where hopes and desires are joyous luxuries
Not the detritus of broken lives

How often have I indulged this fantasy only to be
defeated
Shorn of sustenance in lands of plenty
Nagged by a despairing sense that to lose the bond
With those unfulfilled desires and hopeless expectations
Would be to lose everything

NOTES ON LAND OF UNFULFILLED DESIRES

Title of original: *farsh-e naumiidii-e diidaar*

Translations available in: Khalid Hasan

This version first published: Unpublished

Personal Note: This poem by Faiz reflects the feelings of all those torn between leaving and not leaving, the lingering dilemma of many South Asians.

Stay With Me

My love, my torment
Stay with me

Through the night
That soothes and stabs in turn
Smiles and sobs in turn
Succours and scares in turn

Stay with me
When the night
Disconsolate and mournful
Turns to slip its mooring

Stay constant
My love, my torment
Stay with me

NOTES ON STAY WITH ME

Title of original: *paas raho*

Translations available in: Agha Shahid Ali, Naomi Lazard, Khalid Hasan, Victor Kiernan, Shiv Kumar, Baran Farooqi

This version first published: Unpublished

Personal Note: None

A Prison Morning

Darkness stills the mind
Drawing near in time and space
Fond memories of our homes and loved ones

The time to meditate is over
Even before the dark is spent
Thoughts unravel and dissolve
In confused, ungovernable tumult

Dawn comes upon us like a betrayal
The sun siding with men
Intent on our humiliation

The yard is filled
With noise and cries and quarrels
Men herded like animals without honour
Gathered thoughts scatter like shards
Stab painfully as sudden sword thrusts

Light strips us of our dignity
Yet it does not extend into infinity

NOTES ON A PRISON MORNING

Title of original: *zindaaN kii aik subh*

Translations available in: Agha Shahid Ali, Naomi Lazard, Victor Kiernan, Baran Farooqi

This version first published: Unpublished

Personal Note: This poem came to mind on reading an article by Tim Parks titled 'In the Tumult of Translation' (http://www.nybooks.com/daily/2016/01/19/tumult-of-translation-primo-levi/) in which he discusses Primo Levi's *If This is a Man*. The correspondence in the descriptions of the prison environment were uncanny. I have synthesized the two in the adaptation. It was shared with Tim Parks in order to obtain his permission for publication.

My Visitors

Visitors stream into the storehouse of my sorrows

Evening
Dragging its net of sadness
Night
Spreading darkening tales of woe
Morning
Stabbing wounded memories
Afternoon
Hiding invisible whips

Accomplices of night and day
Visitors arrive, await, go away
My thoughts
Ride waves of fantasy
Homeward bound
Burdened with the weight
Of unanswered questions

NOTES ON MY VISITORS

Title of original: *mere milne waaley*

Translations available in: Naomi Lazard, Khalid Hasan

This version first published: Unpublished

Personal Note: None

Evening

In the passage of the evening
Do you sense an interval
When time is suspended
Enmeshed in a sorcerer's net

Like being entombed in a dark, deserted temple
Whose keeper, smeared in ashes, is bowed in resignation

And then, of a sudden, the moment is past
Life stirs anew, the earth resumes its motion

A song, a bell, a prayer, a knell
The imperceptible nod of an idol's head
A devotee's shy smile of affirmation

NOTES ON EVENING

Title of original: *shaam*

Translations available in: Agha Shahid Ali, Naomi Lazard, Victor Kiernan, Shiv Kumar

This version first published: Unpublished

Personal Note: This poem was brought to mind by a temple visit.

You and I

I saw you once
A lifetime ago
Not a day has passed
I haven't thought of you
Is there a name for a bond like this
Not marked by unions and separations
Not measured in yesterdays and tomorrows
Silent, invisible
Like a river beneath a river
A face behind a face

NOTES ON YOU AND I

Title of original: *jo mera tumhara rishta hai*

Translations available in: Naomi Lazard

This version first published: Unpublished

Personal Note: On reading *The Face Behind the Face: Poems of Yevgeny Yevtushenko.*

Prison Visits

There are some prisoners whom none visit
Except the darkness
That arrives every night
Gorged on the bustle of the day
Bringing both solace and pain
Relief and restlessness

And the one biding its time
To visit just once
Whom we await with longing and fear

NOTES ON PRISON VISITS

Title of original: *mulaqaat miri*

Translations available in: Victor Kiernan

This version first published: Unpublished

Personal Note: On waiting for the one biding its time.

Parting Thoughts

I am curious
How you will recall the past
When I am no more

Longing, remorse, amusement, indifference

Right now I cannot tell
Then I will not care

But would it matter to you
How you will recall the past

NOTES ON PARTING THOUGHTS

Title of original: *akhrii khat*

Translations available in: Agha Shahid Ali, Khalid Hasan

This version first published: Unpublished

Personal Note: This translation of Nazim Hikmet's poem in Turkish into Urdu by Faiz served as the inspiration for my efforts. If one were not informed it was a translation, it would pass as a poem written in Urdu.

Celestial Music

Past and present lie waste
Silenced, stilled
Entombed in dead light
Consumed by forgetfulness

Eternities away, ages ago
Two black holes
Exhale a shudder of ecstasy
Resurrecting life
Awakening dreams and desires
The yearning for beauty and truth

NOTES ON CELESTIAL MUSIC

Title of original: *sarod-e shabaana*

Translations available in: Khalid Hasan, Shiv Kumar

This version first published: Unpublished

Personal Note: The 2016 discovery of gravitational waves brought this poem to mind. Dr. Nergis Mavalvala was one of the scientists on the team at MIT that was associated with the discovery. This poem was dedicated to her and she was kind enough to acknowledge it with the request to use it in one of her lectures.

Do What You Have Left Undone

The world fills up with regrets
By the time you reach a certain age
Even though you are so admired

Like
Why didn't I take mum out the day before she died
Or have dad's cataracts removed in time
Why did I have or not these kids
And provide or not for them a stable home
Why did I consume so much when so many were starving
Why didn't I do more for poverty, injustice and global
warming

True enough
But every moment bears fresh seeds of life
New passions, new affairs begin
Why mourn desires unfulfilled at the end
When still there is so much left to tend

Take your scooter out, put on your helmet
Venture forth for the rendezvous
Who knows what will be lost or won
Smiles come with tears, dreams with fears
Go do what you have to do
Do all that you have left undone

NOTES ON DO WHAT YOU HAVE LEFT UNDONE

Title of original: *tum apnii karnii kar guzro*

Translations available in: Khalid Hasan, Baran Farooqi

This version first published: Unpublished

Personal Note: It was natural to think of this poem as regrets piled up with the passage of time. It was odd to reflect in this state of mind on the 2012 episode involving the French President Francois Hollande who ventured for a tryst on a motor scooter. Perhaps he had the right attitude to life.

You Tell Me What to Do

Loneliness is a dark place
I cradle the embers of distant memories
Hoping a momentary glow would recall
The passion of our union
Afraid that in the ashes
Sinister shadows would wrestle through the restless night

They tell me
It is not brave to nurse the glow of faded memories
I should light a fire instead
That would imbue
My struggle and your sacrifice with greater meaning

You be the judge
You tell me what to do
Forego the sweet pain of accidental meetings
For a fiery embrace that would light up the sky
You tell me what I owe to you

NOTES ON YOU TELL ME WHAT TO DO

Title of original: *dard aaye ga dabbe pa'oN*

Translations available in: Khalid Hasan, Shiv Kumar

This version first published: Unpublished

Personal Note: The perennial dilemma of what to do is a frequent reminder of this poem. Re-reading Albert Hirschman's classic *Exit, Voice, and Loyalty* refreshed its memory.

Love

Let memories flood back if they will
Let wounds reopen if they will
We can continue to meet as strangers
Sitting across from each other for some moments
Enough for me to add up my losses

Our words will bear the burden of what is not said
There will be no mention of promises kept or broken
If the past becomes evident in my eyes
You may please to read or not to read them
And the feelings that arise in your heart
You may please to express or not to express them

NOTES ON LOVE

Title of original: *koi aashiq kisii mehbooba se*

Translations available in: Naomi Lazard, Khalid Hasan, Shiv
Kumar, Baran Farooqi

This version first published: Unpublished

Personal Note: Anyone who has been through the ups and downs
of a long relationship will think of this poem by Faiz more than
once.

All or Nothing

Every breath is due to you
Every word is due to you

We have fallen on bad days, it's true
Love, beauty, truth, all lie askew

But what of that, but what of that
One day the buds will bloom anew

Were I to listen to my head
Won't we be as good as dead

NOTES ON ALL OR NOTHING

Title of original: *sabhii kuchh hai*

Translations available in: Khalid Hasan

This version first published: Unpublished

Personal Note: This is the one ghazal in this collection.

Voice

You don't see me
Are you blind
Or do I not exist
Open your eyes
Let your gaze be interrupted by my face
Let us fashion a world that has place for both of us
Our voices will carry further
There will be an echo
That will reveal the mysteries of the universe

NOTES ON VOICE

Title of original: *mire dard ko jo zubaaN mile*

Translations available in: Naomi Lazard, Shiv Kumar, Baran Farooqi

This version first published: Unpublished

Personal Note: The yearning for an inclusive society brought this poem to mind.

A Special Love

What am I to you
You to me
Which chapter of the book of love
Will own our story
This undeclared passion
Neither union nor separation
Just an ache
A constant reminder that something special is at stake

NOTES ON A SPECIAL LOVE

Title of original: *jo mera tumhaara rishta hai*

Translations available in: Naomi Lazard

This version first published: Unpublished

Personal Note: A reflection on relationships.

Loss

I seek the word
That embodies my thought to perfection
So that a beautiful act
Emerges from the thought of beauty
And the thought of devastation
Implodes before it becomes a fact

Alas, the note is false
The instrument is out of tune
The voice wavers in search of tact
This is a time when anything will soothe
A screech, a scream, a broken pact
There is no call to be exact

NOTES ON LOSS

Title of original: *aaj ek harf ko phir DhuunDta phirta hai khayal*

Translations available in: Khalid Hasan, Baran Farooqi

This version first published: Unpublished

Personal Note: The dawn of the era of post-truth brought this poem to mind.

Hope

There are times
When everyone, everything, exists for itself
The moon refuses to share its light
Stars recede into their black holes
Mirrors swallow their images
Even lovers fail to turn up for their trysts

What does it mean to hope in such times
Who would one turn to and for what
Faith would only call forth deception

Let such times pass
The moon will yearn for the admiring gaze
Stars will pine to light the way
Mirrors will invite the longing look
Lovers will crave the warm embrace

Amidst the nods of recognition
Hope will find its place again

NOTES ON HOPE

Title of original: *kahaaN jaaoge*

Translations available in: Khalid Hasan, Shiv Kumar

This version first published: Unpublished

Personal Note: None

This Moment

The earth stopped spinning on its axis
The mind blanked out, dreams disappeared
No faces were recognized, no ties remembered
And all the pain in the world found a home in the heart

The sounds I seemed to sense
Were those of existence ebbing out of my pores

How odd then that if I survive this moment
Life would resume as if nothing had happened

NOTES ON THIS MOMENT

Title of original: *is waqt to yuuN lagta hai*

Translations available in: Naomi Lazard, Khalid Hasan, Shiv Kumar

This version first published: Unpublished

Personal Note: A reflection on the meaninglessness of one's life.

Revolt

Nights of pain
Days in vain
An endless circle of despair
Is this what you term as fair

I hear them say
This is your way
You're compassionate and just
You manage every speck of dust

Take your pick but I am loath
I'll give you one but never both

NOTES ON REVOLT

Title of original: *mazluum*

Translations available in: Khalid Hasan

This version first published: Unpublished

Personal Note: This is part two of Faiz's 'Three Voices' - a reflection on our present-day dialogue of the deaf.

The End

What would the end be like

Sweet and lingering
Like the culmination of an unexpected kiss
Warm and reluctant
Like the morning after a night of shared memories
Brutal and merciless
Like a pestilence sweeping across the earth's crust

Who knows what the end would be like
And does it matter
As random as the beginning that brought us into the world

It was only in the passing we clawed back some order from
the randomness
Imbued a sense of meaning to our living and loving
So that we may have no regrets when the end arrived

NOTES ON THE END

Title of original: *jis roz qaza aaegii*

Translations available in: Naomi Lazard, Khalid Hasan, Baran
Farooqi

This version first published: Unpublished

Personal Note: The thought of why one should care how death
will come brought this poem by Faiz to mind.